SIGNS FOR AN EXHIBITION

SIGNS FOR AN EXHIBITION

Poems by ELIZA KENTRIDGE

Published in 2015 by Modjaji Books
PO Box 121, Rondebosch, 7701, Cape Town, South Africa
www.modjajibooks.co.za

© 2015 Eliza Kentridge
ISBN 978-1-920590-79-6
e-book ISBN 978-1-928215-04-2

Book and cover design: Oliver Barstow
Cover artwork: Eliza Kentridge
Editor: Joan Metelerkamp

Printed and bound by Megadigital.

For my parents

SIGN POEM 1

The shadow of olive leaves on the wall

HOUSE FOR SALE

Light from the water shimmering on the buildings

SPACE TO RENT

The soft rain of summer

POET FOR HIRE

WHERE ARE YOU?

A cat stretched on a hot stone step

I'M CALLING

Jasmine and bougainvillea round the door

DO YOU HEAR ME?

The smell of jasmine

I'M LISTENING

Lanterns rising above the bay

Very high near the moon

IMPERTURBABLE

Moonlight dividing the sea

DANCING EVERY SATURDAY

Swallows flit softly through the house

TENNIS ON SUNDAYS

Peaches ripening in a blue bowl

TEMPORARY HAPPINESS

Long hoped for calm

EMOTIONAL TECHNOLOGY

Yesterday, today and tomorrow

THE MECHANICS OF THE HEARTSTRINGS

I wanted to ask you

ARE YOU ALRIGHT?

I wanted to tell you

IT WILL BE ALRIGHT

Flat on your back on the dry wintry grass

The sun on your face

Ants whispering in your ears

YOU'RE HOME, YOU'RE HOME

Chickens twisting on rotisseries

Snow on eastern fields

THE TRAIN APPROACHES THE CITY

A timely arrival

This is the world as we know it

DESERTIFICATION

HYDROLOGY

PIXELLATION

We have come to a virtual standstill

HUMMINGBIRD AND MORNING GLORY

Housewives run through the streets

I STROKE YOUR HEAD

China tea last thing before bed

I HOLD YOUR HAND

Summer lightning above the hills

I GUESS YOUR THOUGHTS

Cradled by a stranger

(LET ME CRADLE YOU)

All the sights in the world ache for your eyes

AM I RIGHT?

The eye a delta of veins

THUMBS UP IF I'M RIGHT

Your heart in your mouth

Sun coming up over the Karoo

DON'T FRET

Wet brush licking the paint

THERE IS ENOUGH LOVE

There is more than enough love

SIGN POEM 2

THIS BOOK WILL SHOCK YOU!

KEEP OFF THE GRASS!

So underdressed that first winter in Oxford

So cold on the bike, everything new and hard

THE LAYOUT OF THE HEART

The raggedy bone shop of the heart

Deserts seen from the air

THAT BOY!

HE COULD WORK A ROOM

Not shy in the corner like some I could name

Grand pianos in heavenly houses

Groceries balanced from handlebars

Delicate imperfections

Bright oranges on a poor table

Your face reflected in the window

Soft coloured Oxford stone

WE NEEDED ALL THE HELP WE COULD GET

Wilting tulips a lovely scrawl

EYES ON THE HORIZON

Hands on the wheel

The wind in the blue gum trees

HOW IT USED TO BE

Hand on heart

All ears

Naked in Laingsburg

WHO WERE YOU?

Unspeaking

Grass bangles rattling my wrist

WHAT DID YOU WANT?

The blood in my veins

Windows lit up along the parade

HOW IT IS NOW

Far away hands waving

The past trailing behind you like an angel

I MUST BE SOME KIND OF IDIOT

Light on the wine glasses

ARE YOU STILL SEWING?

I can't

My fucking hands are broken

SIGN POEM 3

Abject dogs squat behind pillars
We avert our eyes

Subject/abject

Transient beauty
Temporary happiness

WHERE IS THE CHILD YOU ONCE WERE?

Yachts swing on their buoys
Swans bounce over the swell
Approach with caution

THE WIND HAS GONE FROM MY SAILS

Swans bounce gently over the swell

IS THERE SOMETHING IN YOUR EYE?

The river like pewter
Like a memory
Clear in the middle, cloudy at the edges

Bread burns in the hot cage of the toaster
The words catch in your throat
The wind ruffles your hair

HOW COULD WE HAVE KNOWN?

Your trousers give birth to your socks
WHERE'VE YOU BEEN?

Southern Cross and Northern Lights
White doves wheeling from the roof

WHERE'VE YOU BEEN?

SIGN POEM 4

Winter grass
Dry yellow spikes pricking my soles
Something set tingling
Erotic shoots

SUPPER'S READY
COMING
COME NOW. SUPPER'S READY
I SAID I'M COMING

The rug dragged in from the lawn
Dead leaves in the hall
Quick, before the storm
Badminton rackets chucked beneath the stairs
Little cave of cricket bats and electrical wiring

The sky green

DO WE LIVE IN AN ENGLISH BOOK?

The dalmation from next door comes over
Balls like huge hail stones
Our own dog a mess of wounds
(Skulking in after a fight)
We spend shameful hours at the vet
The dog like something off a butcher's slab

OUT OF THE POOL
THERE'S LIGHTNING
BUT IT'S FAR AWAY
OUT NOW

Orange cat leaping to its death on Louis Botha
Feral kittens on the corner
Hair plaited for school
And now my own girls

LOOK AT THE STATE OF IT
DO YOU NEVER BLOODY BRUSH IT?

Fine embroidery on the school blouse
Fine embroidery on my grandmother's napkins
Fine embroidery on the maid's bedspread
Stitched late at night after the dishes
And still needles pricking my own fingers

CAN YOU REALLY NOT REMEMBER?

Sweat under your arms
Blood on the sheets
Twenty four hours of crying

THEY WERE THE NASTY GIRLS

And the nice ones
And the boys

DON'T FORGET THE BOYS

Yoga after school
Fish in a bowl swimming to Patti Smith
Smoky winter dusk
The world had to begin somewhere
Love had to come from somewhere

ORTHODONTIST
ART CLASSES
HOMEWORK

The gables, the rose garden, the main hall
Horrid matron dispensing clothes
Dispensing with kindness
Gone like the cat on the road
And less mourned

TENNIS AGAIN AND AGAIN
SWIMMING THE ENDLESS WATERWAYS
UNTIL YOU DROWN

DID I SAY YOU COULD STOP, ELIZABETH?

Pebbles ripping through my tights
Embedded in my six-year-old knee
Don't cry, they'll laugh
The knees that didn't meet so they laughed

YOU LITTLE STOIC

Like later on a trampoline outside Washington
Feeling my back almost snap

NEVER TOLD
PARENTS NEVER KNEW

Though I was almost crippled
Still damaged
They never knew

WERE YOU MAD?

Syringa trees, agapanthus

SUPPER'S UP
OKAY COMING

Now the children pick my brains
They pick at my life like grapes off a bunch
My life is like an outdated machine
They help install the upgrades

WHO WERE YOU?

Not yet their mother
Not yet loved
Waiting for the grand event

Localised ennui

INTERNATIONAL YEARNING

The same crush year after year after year
In the bath legs so perfect
Shape and line undented by hockey bruises
But he neither knew nor cared

Prickly grass fucking my soles
Early needles pricking my fingers
Sailor suits for kittens
Satin nighties for dolls
A cushion for the grandparents
Bargello details for the murdered teacher

But you, mother of mine
YOU KINDLY SEWED UP MY KNITTED DALMATION
Soft and suitably gelded

THANK YOU
THANK YOU FOR HAVING ME

Risible
Derisory

CHILDREN NEED NOT THANK PARENTS FOR HAVING THEM

Rose beetles crashing into night-time walls
Crickets leaping up from the bush
Mulberries, figs, hibiscus
Blackjacks, red ants

The humming backdrop to our lives
And you our queen bee
A great achiever

A PERSON OF SPLENDOUR

All the beauties rolled into one
Men unable to eat at sparkling tables
Silenced in meetings
Dropping by to mend the fridge
For a glance from your almond eyes

The girls have your eyes
One the shape
One the colour
And the boy your nose
And all of them your apt words

WE CLAIM YOU

Laughing so much that day the big man sat on the small man
You laughed all the way home
Piccadilly Line to Sandwich Street
Sharing the little squashed man
The oblivious bulk on top of him
The whole carriage shaking with silent laughter
The tube exploding with laughter
Great shared fun
The little man none the worse for wear
His paper rather crumpled

WE COULD ALL LAUGH SO MUCH

Late night gossip over tea
China tea, with jasmine blossom
Black stools round the yellow kitchen table
Pecking at cake and stories
Gathering the different evenings into one

GOODNIGHT
GOODNIGHT

And still
Even in recent times
Dad's Army, 'Allo, 'Allo
They've done it for you

OH MUM YOU'RE LAUGHING

Even with language fled

THUMBS UP IF YOU'RE LAUGHING
Even with the words stopped on your tongue
Even with your eyes turned away
Your body unable
Unable
But cupped in cushions and loving arms
Even and despite

THE JOKE FINDS YOU

The joke is not on you
It is in you

SIGN POEM 5

From highveld to riverbed
South to East
Africa to Anglia
Not in the blink of an eye
Not at the flick of a switch
But the change was effected
The transition completed
City afternoons to village mornings

The deceptive green of winter grass
A cap of green for the earth's muddied scalp
And where were the dry blades of home?

BUT THIS IS HOME

IT TAKES SO LONG TO GET HOME

It takes no time at all
It's a bus ride
Just run over the bridge
Down that lane
You're there
Next to the train tracks

From the ridge of white waters
To the bridge over the line

SIGN POEM 6

The dawn roll-call of wild dogs
Ears round as spoons
Gathering near the Land Rover
In Mickey Mouse hats

RARE TO SEE SO MANY

Bumping through undergrowth
Acacias, thickets of thorns
Impalas skittering, guinea fowl quecking
Branches slashing at outstuck elbows

SSH I THOUGHT I SAW A LION

Banging on the roof for the driver to stop
No-one breathe

THERE NEAR THE ANTHILL, UNDER THE TREE

It was true

HOW LUCKY WE ARE, WHAT LUCK

Another time hippos
Okavango delta, hippos round the boat
Fish leaping for the line
Tiger fish that is

Inedible
And you in the orange and black striped shirt
Indelible
Kingfishers in the reeds and of course snouts of crocodiles

DON'T TRAIL YOUR FINGERS

And another word to the wise

IF A HIPPO CHARGES, RUN UP A TREE

Never forget

I NEVER WILL
NEVER HAVE

Besides us, you loved Roberts Birds of South Africa
Travelling watercolours
Updike under the mosquito net

Years later, our own tiny ones attached like monkeys
We walked through Zimbabwean bush
The long, long grasses near a lake
A mother rhino and her baby feeding
Our hearts uplifted and terrified
Mostly terrified

JUST KEEP WALKING, DON'T SPEAK

A story now for English tables
You did such a lot of driving
All those holidays to Kruger, the Drakensberg

Dawn starts
The sun a sudden red ball
Sackfuls of roadside oranges
And all the roadside people
Walking impossible miles

WHAT BRINGS US TO THIS PRETTY PASS?

Bitter green oil from the oranges
Kneading and kneading them
Papercuts stinging from the intaglio oil
Instructions from big sister and brother

MAKE A HOLE IN THE SKIN
NO, LIKE THIS
NOW SUCK

Lying sticky with juice on a blanket
Littlies freestyle in the boot
Sky and telephone wires lifting and falling
How do the cloud animals change so slowly?
Watching with infinite acceptance until sleepy
Nauseous

STOP THE CAR, STOP RIGHT NOW

Somewhere near Mount Sheba
Sardines and apples beside a stream
Running water so we could wade

IT'S OKAY, DON'T THINK THERE'S BILHARZIA

Blood dripping from your gashed thumb
The penknife's elegant treachery

LET ME LOOK, DAD

We tended you then
You pale and shocked
The river running clear over stones

Mount Sheba
The pretty rounded hills were Sheba's breasts
Thatched rondavels and a ping pong room
Our waiter in a red fez and sash

CAN I HAVE A LIME JUICE AND SODA?
WHERE'S THE PLEASE?
PLEASE

Such glittering cold stars on the walk back from supper
Your thumb swaddled

WHO WANTS A CHAPTER?
US, US
WE ALL DO

There was always a book on the go
I fell asleep to Dickens and Nesbit
Year after year in the feathered room of your voice

IT'S REALLY BEDTIME NOW

Small ones shivering happily in blanketed bunks
Parents' voices rising up under the thatch
You bandaged, wounded

It must have hurt

You went similarly pale
Forty years later beside a Sussex priory
Scotch eggs
Stories of loving daughters, Lear
Wife, children, grandchildren
Hot coffee under the oaks
All stretched and disporting
Cake
But you were got by a bee
Or an English wasp

Huge agony in your hand
We all felt it

LET ME SEE, DAD

A pond, reeds, rosy crumbling bricks
Birdsong
Honeysuckle

YOU NEED AN ANTIHISTAMINE

The baby dandled on a soft lap
Transcontinental cousins gathered in a ball

IT FEELS LIKE I WAS STABBED

All of us put out with the bee
The picnic packed away
Our anger with the bee quite real
Your anxiety palpable
We made a protective swarm around you

HAVE THIS CHOCOLATE, DAD
YOU NEED SUGAR

I knew a wasp once
I put my unwitting childhood hand
On its maroon wasp-waist
And its needle pricked me til I screamed
You brought purple spirits of ammonia
Good also for washing hairbrushes
The wasp dead on the sill
The dot left by its sword visible in my fat, etherised palm

A distraction:
LET'S LOOK AT THE TREES

Through layers of tears and casement glass
Looking down at the avenues of jacarandas
I noticed how the jacaranda blossom and the stinking ammonia

Were almost the same colour
All my life I have loved those trees

We take comfort where we find it

SIGN POEM 7

Here is the dirt road where my days are spent
Drawn margin of the village
Stage and playground for half my life
Quite surprising when you think about it
The surprise of landing up
The surprise of where life spills you and where you hang on

ARCHAEOLOGICAL TIME

A Victorian road running from farm to river
Crossing a railway line running from London to the sea

UP AND DOWN THE CITY ROAD
IN AND OUT THE EAGLE

Marshlands here and the famous wide sky

RESIDENTS PARKING ONLY

Though everyone parks as they please

20 MILES PER HOUR
CHILDREN PLAYING

And so are summer sparrows in hollows full of dust

All this English ease of access to wetlands and the sea
While I come from dry uplands in another hemisphere
In my dreams we are on the koppie

Lizards resting on hot stones
Johannesburg opening out to the north a sea of trees
In the distance the Magaliesberg

TO HELL AND GONE

ON A HIDING TO NOTHING

HALF WAY TO VOETSAK

Here Victorian builders came to work
Moleskin trousers and tiny clay pipes
They dug these earth foundations, handbuilt this terrace
Meat pies and ale at a pub near the shipyard
Johannesburg still a mote in its mother's eye

This row built for ships' captains
A terrace gently hoiking itself up the hill
Sail lofts, fireplaces, sash windows
While there – scrubby veld and ridges of rock
Gold unbothered in the ground
Lizards above, and eagles, a variety of buck
Meerkats
Quite possibly leopards

WHAT POWERS OF RECALL

And then the whole history
A whole city conjured into being
A whole society dug from the earth

AM I RIGHT?

Meanwhile here the village carried on
People wandered up this same road to the farm

SIMULTANEOUS HISTORY

SPONTANEOUS COMBUSTION

A ship built for the Prince of Wales
Railings carted off to make World War guns
The river rising and falling in its tides
Sheep grazing and bleating
Shorebirds tracking the water's edge

WE HAVE BEEN THROWN BACKWARDS

I know dirt roads in the south

The road to Retief's Kloof
Beyond the padlocked gate
The huge boulders we slid down into the rock pool
And the view over beloved Transvaal bush

HOW I MISS THE BUNDU

Orange roads through green Transkei landscapes
Dongas and ruts chopping the surface
Our car's shock absorber bent double
But a man under a tree fixed it
Took it off and bashed it straight on the selfsame tree

RIGHT AS RAIN
HOW CAN WE THANK HIM?

Money of course and memory
The car fine for years after that

YOU'LL NEVER BELIEVE WHAT HAPPENED

It got us down the buckled road to the sea
Tropical fields giving way to a blanket of blue
Great miles of sand laid on for us
Thin boys and their cattle wandering through the foam
A mirage approaching til they passed
Big smiles and waves, huge humpnecked Afrikanders
Horns spreading wide, ribs

Another car story
Remember that time after the game reserve?
Something wrong with the engine
All of us piled out on the roadside like luggage
Various useless attempts at tinkering

WHAT DO LAWYERS KNOW ABOUT ENGINES?

Our family friend lolling on the verge
Novel in hand
Pale American in a hat
The most useless of the lot

OH YE OF LITTLE FAITH

At the appointed time
Known only to himself
He rose
Placed his hands upon the engine
And fie! The bloody thing started

SHYSTERS THE LOT OF THEM

That road down to the river at a Knysna farm
Hanging on in the back of a 4 x 4
Wheels skimming the edge of a ravine
Fragile trees, almost a rainforest, filling the hollow
Imaginably crushable were we to fall
Would they catch us if we fell?

DON'T LOOK
I WANT TO LOOK

The bakkie jolting over boulders and roots
We are side by side with precipitous death
Holding on by our fingertips
The sun burning our noses

NOW THAT'S WHAT I CALL A GOOD ROAD
MY FAVOURITE KIND OF ROAD

With a river at the bottom
Crickets and birds loud in the heat
A wild fig to shade the rugs
Then running over sharp pebbles to the brown shallows

Wafting in layered currents
Cliff jumpers splashing in near a canoe
The scene lapped into camera screens and phones

COME OUT NOW
YOU'RE GETTING BURNED

Hats, sunscreen

YOU'RE ALREADY BURNED

All those years of craziness
Frying up like a full English next to the pool
Lobsterine on the beach
Shoulders peeling in layers like mica
And now the mottled damage
Fearful checking of moles, molehills

BUT THE ENGLISH WOMEN!

What fine and creamy skin
Skin stretched softly over breastbones
Cheeks younger than their years
Necks plump and uncrabbed
Ripe for vampires

I COULD KISS YOU NOW

A rough boy once lay beside the pool
My truanting neighbour

A cigarette for homework
Smoking hot in the heat

A SNAKE CAME TO MY WATER TROUGH

And I, not pyjama'd
But cased in navy tunic and brown socks
Stupid hat stuffed between books
His blatant disregard for rules
My primly ruffled sensibility

I AM AFFRONTED SAID MRS TIGGYWINKLE

NOBODY SHOULD BE ALONE AT THE POOL

Him sizzling rudely in trunks
The pine trees and bougainvillea reflected in blue water
Me speechless at the cheek of him
Me speechless at the sight of him
Or is that the trick of years?

So troubled a boy, it must be said

I DIDN'T KNOW YOU

Motorbikes roaring all night
Racing in the dark down the jacaranda avenue
I wished them dead
Vicious tripwires in my head
And then one died
Turns out he was your friend

I'M SORRY

I had no idea of my own power

SIGN POEM 8

FILIGREE OF NERVES
FILIGREE OF VINES
MUSICAL NOTATION OF DAMAGE

Bird leaping up for lard ball suspended from the branch
Snow flying down from spring skies
Daffodils struggling to make themselves heard

IN MY HEAD YOUR HEAD

Genomic structure of the tau gene
Sparrow replaced by bobbing robin
Deposition of hyperphosphorylated tau
Leafbuds on the lilac stymied for another day

Big brown starling sends the robin away
Red breast heaving

NEURODEGENERATIVE DISORDERS

PATHOLOGICAL HALLMARKS

My own breast heaves at times

I read this thing about your thing
In medical language it described your brain
The tendrils choking neural pathways
The vines which tangle the knowledge you contain
All that you contain we still know

You contain more than we could ever know

YOUR EYES REACH TO US ACROSS THE LEAVES

More birds arrive
They pick nuts through the mesh bag strung from a branch
The mindfulness of a neighbour
Little living creatures stumbling through another winter

NORTHERN WINTRY DESOLATION

IN THE SOUTH IT IS ALWAYS SUMMER
IT IS ASSUMED
SO THEY SAY

This thing: PSP
The sibilance of suffering
P.S. it's PSP
It is whispered

Hummingbirds make signs in your brain
Morning glories flower among your thoughts
Progressive Supranuclear Palsy
A mind in sliced photographs

IT IS CONFIRMED

A multitude of birds in our southern garden
Hadedas in the undergrowth
Piet-my-vrous calling through the dusk
Hoopoes, doves

The cat's gift of a writhing pigeon
Special delivery under the dining room table
Its yellow eye and red blood stark against the parquet
My contribution to the meal said the polite cat
Flying ants spinning through the darkening garden
The sky green after the storm
Then shading into black
Cats beautifully twisting to catch the ants

GOD THEY'RE IN MY HAIR

The dim suggestion of feasting bats
We close windows and doors
In the morning the ants' cellophane wings all over the floor
The broom set to work

Did we have hummingbirds?
Five thousand feet above sea level
A temperate zone
I think not
They flutter and hover in the New World

LET ME STROKE YOUR HEAD

What do I know?

DON'T MIND ME
MIND THE GAP

Rosy-faced lovebirds at Johannesburg Zoo
Their cage just past the turnstile
Green feathers and the red cheeks of love
The fine whirligig of candyfloss

BUT GRAMPA WE'RE NOT ALLOWED
IT'S ALRIGHT
I WON'T TELL

Near disaster at the pelican cage
My short finger poking through the wire
The short pelican lunging
Grown-up claws grabbing me back
It would have pocketed my finger
Trousered the change
The greedy handbag of its beak still looms

HOW SMALL WE WERE
SLOW-WITTED WITH YOUTH

The nursery school outing
Shyly dumb in the back of a mother's car

COULD YOU OPEN THE WINDOW PLEASE, MY GIRL?

I pull at a likely lever
The door flies open above the rushing road
Grown-up mitts grabbing me back from my death tumble

DON'T CALL ME MY GIRL
I DON'T EVEN KNOW YOU

Those whimpering nursery days
My arms stretching out to stop him going
DADDY, DADDY
Kind hands pulling me firmly back
Sandwiches with jam
The agony of telling them, day after day
I DON'T LIKE JAM
The lispy whisper of a shy child

WHY COULD THEY NEVER REMEMBER?

All I wanted was to be at home
In the garden
In the cave on the koppie
With my dolls and cats
Pine trees towering above
Later a Marie biscuit on your lap
On the verandah under the Bauhinia
Its tendrils dropping down
Its bell flowers a bower for our heads
Velvety, sunset-coloured flowers
Just made for a long beak, a chameleon's tongue, a child's finger

Wisteria drapes a London courtyard
Your lap draped in a russet blanket

YOU KNEW YOUR OWN MIND

Always the question of tenses

We dangled a string for a dancing kitten
Safe and happy
The air warm and filled with birdsong

The world broke my heart even then

SIGN POEM 9

There's that waking from a dream
Having found the thing one had lost
Like tonight
It was there, my lost glove
Crushed in the wet road
I was so happy to retrieve it

Often you come to us in our dreams
You are better
You can walk, speak
We go to the opera
We embrace

GIVE ME A HUG
YOU'VE BEEN GONE SO LONG

Sometimes you are rising from the table
From your table
As you naturally did

Waking from the dreams of finding
I lie for a moment
Information gathers itself around me
Shifting clumps of quicksilver
My body mantled with its phosphorescence
Like a swimmer in a night sea

WHAT DOES IT MEAN?

The meaning clears momentarily
It gathers to an image
The lost glove found
The sick one cured

A TEMPORARY TRUTH

Then the crystals shift again
The lens refracts again
Washed again in the old knowledge
Glove still lost
You afflicted still

I tried to catch my dream glove in words written at a window
A full moon shone on my pencil
Silently pencilling so as not to wake the sleeper
Big moon over the river and the fields
Half naked and shivering
The scene quite Japanese

YOU REALLY LIKED HOKUSAI

Turning the big pages on the window seat
The wave and Mount Fuji spread across our laps

In the dream I had come out of a house
Turned back for a glimpse of its lit windows

Red satin upholstery, tassels
Unfamiliar, gorgeously formal
But I knew the house

The scene quite Chinese

A woman sat, her back to the window
I wanted to ask her

WHO ARE YOU?

Then I saw the glove in the dark street
A leather hand flattened under car wheels
My hand
I picked it up so I could mend it
Put my hand back in my pocket where it belongs

WE MUST MEND OUR WAYS

In my dreams, you are trying to walk
Edging past people to your seat at the opera
I support you
You crumple against me
We make it to our seats
You loved many operas but not Wagner
You love many operas but not Wagner

WHAT TENSE ARE YOU USING, ELIZABETH?

You hate Lieder
Your sweeping pronouncements

Comically wrinkled nose
That pretty neat nose you did not give me

I NEVER WANT TO SEE ANOTHER MADAM BUTTERFLY

A Sussex table
Sun coming in through Georgian windows
Inside the walls are dappled with leaf shadows
Inlaid mirrors reflect roses, sky, clouds, the striped lawn
Roasted platters are carried in

CAN YOU MOVE UP A BIT, PLEASE?

A grandmother's embroidered napkin at every place
We drank water from these pewter beakers in a former life
Such ages ago

WHO WOULD HAVE THOUGHT IT?

Bread from the farm shop

SHALL I CARVE?
WHICH BIT DO YOU LIKE?
I'M A BREAST MAN MESELF

Green curtains sink richly to the floor
Food sinking richly down our throats
A modicum of wine
Of course chocolate afterwards with the demitasses
Cafetiere tilting drowsily among the grass stalks

WATCH OUT, IT'S SPILLING

Freezing Johannesburg nights
A flannel nightie, drowsy before the fire
Two squares of Cadburys before bed

UP TO BED NOW
CAN'T WE HAVE FIVE MORE MINUTES?
UP YOU GO
I'M COMING TO KISS YOU

Now I am the one who comes up to kiss you
I drop kisses on your brushed head
You groan
My hand smoothes your brow

SSH, SLEEP NOW

London curtains sink richly to the floor

I'LL SEE YOU IN THE MORNING

A Johannesburg table
Round as a coin
But we all knew our place
The groaning board, the Mexican candlestick
We fed well
All those years of our growing

My own children less well
An Essex table, tulips dropping petals

COULD THEY NOT EAT AIR?

Rugs spread under the apple trees
A baby spread on my chest
You bring a tray
You are mothering me into motherhood
Scones
Local cherry jam

THIS IS AN ENGLISH BOOK

Buttercups at eye level
Ants, sunbefokked bees
Soil in heaps on the mossy grass

THE MOLES ARE BACK
IRREPRESSIBLE
THE BUGGERS

Little creatures going about their day

Dylan Thomas
A matric question
Now as I was young and easy
A trick question
Under the apple boughs
In truth I knew nothing of apple boughs
But I know them now
About the lilting house
I know the house you mean

AND HAPPY AS THE GRASS WAS GREEN

My baby and I
All the babies under the apple boughs
And all our yesterdays

You in a rustling silk dress for the opera
Scones rustled up
Chicken with apricots in the wide Spanish dish

SHOULD WE HAVE SOME MORE WINE?

On your knees weeding in grief
The pre-millennium summer
A sister's grief
For hours, the beds picked clean
You could have stripped the very lawn to its marrow

You lost your pendant
The faceted crystal drop you loved
We helped you search among the beds
The rose bushes, the grass roots, the mole tunnels
Under the apple boughs
The garden had swallowed it
We were frantic to find it, to help you

I'LL JUST POP OUT FOR ANOTHER LOOK
BUT IT'S ALMOST DARK

No matter
And no luck
It was gone as your sister was gone
Irretrievable

I still potter about the edges of rosebeds, even now
Hoping for a glimpse of a glint
Light refracted from a precious treasure
It MUST be here somewhere
Things outlast people

YOUR EYES AND FINGERS FIND MINE
FIND ME, THEY SAY

If they say that
Do they say that?
We never stop hoping, do we?

SIGN POEM 10

Mevrou clicks past on her tipped stilettos
The sound familiar and chilling
Along the red polished floors of the school corridors
Black men in blue overalls on their knees with polishing cloths

Arranged in rows, arrayed in delft gingham
We watch from our clattering desks

LIKE A WEANED CHILD IS MY SOUL WITHIN ME

You had to come to school with me every day for months
Every day, quiet at the back in your work clothes
Italian shoes and perfect tights
The teacher in her clear stockings
Hairs snaking in ugly legions down her legs

You had to stay for an hour until I settled
Stopped crying
Writing numbers in gingham books
One number per square, no overlapping

NEATLY, ELIZABETH

Checking over my shoulder you were still there

LIKE A WEANED CHILD WITH ITS MOTHER

You left discreetly
A small wave and a nod to the teacher
My lip trembling
Madam's accent a Scottish distraction

SHALL WE HAVE A SONG?

Your life took you elsewhere
It had to
Back in the red-floored corridors we line up
Hymn practice and formation marching

The men in blue overalls smile at the little girls
They are kind and patient
Now tending the roses in the quadrangle
But often they've had to clean up after us
Mouldering lunches
Pools of sudden vomit
The unmanaged puking of children

Like drunks, but too small to be drunk

Bugs made us sick
And so did the head
Mevrou in her black-bunned lair
The witch will see you now
Chucking up outside her door
A minor infraction

The Margot Fonteyn of witches

Letters home
A mine of information
Best wishes from the best of witches

I WISH YOU HADN'T SAID THAT
I WISH I COULD FORGET

Here the children went up the dirt road
We wended our winding way up past the farm
Past the field
Big houses on one side, with big windows
On the other side more fields
Horses, cows, the stripe of the train
The shining bends of the river running to its delta
Across the water the quarry
Its barges plying up and down to London

WHAT ARE YOU IMPLYING?

We live in an English book
We go to school in a Breughel painting
Beat that Johannesburg
Beat that my pretty alma mater

Grampa at the door

BOKER TOV EVERYBODY
BOKER TOV GRAMPA

Hebrew greeting from Tswana Ellen
She hooks his boiled egg out of the bubbling pot
His gift was the drive to school
My parents still luxuriously horizontal

BOKER TOV MY PARENTS

Kneeling beside your sleeping shapes
My goodbyes and entreaties
Plaited
Plaintive

CAN'T I STAY HOME?
MY THROAT IS SO SORE
COUGH COUGH

A mumbled response
OFF YOU GO DARLING

His perspiring Peugeot trundling up the steeps of Munro Drive

Here we walked up the reflective road to a modest school
Big puddles filming the sky

Greetings from the friendly headmaster
Children clamouring around him
Tai chi and motorbikes in his spare time

DO YOU KNOW HOW LUCKY YOU ARE?
ALWAYS REMEMBER THIS

The droned catechism
The luck of the farm, the river, the kind school

BUT I HAVE STILLED AND QUIETED MY SOUL

Repeat after me

BUT I HAVE STILLED AND QUIETED MY SOUL
But I have stilled and quieted my soul

That's good

I used to walk under eucalyptus trees to the rounders field
We learned tikkie draai and langarm dans aged six
I thought I was Francoise Hardy
I thought I would conduct orchestras
Johannesburg traffic roared outside the gates
I thought everyone else had the answer
Days began early
It felt like they would never end

SIGN POEM 11

Rain is falling in north-east Essex
Dampening the dirt road, its ruts and upheavals
Muddy streams running downhill

WITH HEY, HO, THE WIND AND THE RAIN

We used to wait for the spring rains
Waking in the night to the awaited downpour
Stretching and shifting in the satisfied bed
In the morning sharp yellow spikes already softening to green
The lawn a sudden silvered marsh

That's how it was down Johannesburg way

There was a recipe for apple strudel
Elaborate canapés
Index cards written in your just married writing
Unfinished, unbegun
Hatchling brides took lessons then

I imagine your initiated beauty
A fifties kitchen
Formica, culinary wallpaper
An older person's house
Gloves and hat put to one side
Apron pinnied over a tailored dress

LET'S GET TO WORK, GIRLS

Excited laughter and the whisking of egg whites

Some of the cards were well-used
The strudel, for instance
Pancakes
Boeuf bourguignon
The cards smeared and tattered
Butter fingers tracing a path through the years

Others still pristine, barely attempted
Trays of hors d'oeuvres, cunningly conjured
The horrors of gelatine moulds
Liver patties

YOU ARE MAKING THIS UP
UP TO YOUR EYEBALLS IN CORNICHONS

Your hair falling from its web of pins
A dab of flour on your chin
Lips still red and laughing
Feet slightly aching in their arches
Your floury allure
A flower among flowers
Too clever to cook

Driving home to husbands, the brides
Perhaps through a summer storm
Burnt offering in foil on the passenger seat

HUSBAND COMES HOME WITH TICKETS FOR THE BEDROOM

The recipes came to life in other hands
Became oracles for Ellen
Our lady of the kitchen
And for me
I learned at her knee

The mysteries of the strudel
Card propped against the kettle
Pastry rolled thin across the marble counter
Our brown and white hands together on the rolling pin
Cold butter
Pastry stretched out in a tender sheet
My striped apron, her pink uniform
Apples piled in the middle, raisins
The sides folded over, pinched together
Leaves cut and pressed into the strudel's soft body
Painting on eggwash

Through the kitchen window, rain falling on the koppie
Kitty on the windowsill watching the raindrops
Our hands light and dark lifted the baking tray
Me on tiptoes to see into the oven
Flour everywhere

WHAT'S FOR SUPPER?
WAIT AND SEE!

England brought out the cook in you

BY ORDER OF HER MAJESTY THE QUEEN

Trussing quails and poaching trout
An eighties kitchen
Inside steam condenses on a shuttered window
Outside the grey London rain streams down

FOR THE RAIN IT RAINETH EVERY DAY

Geraniums on the vestigial balcony
Plane trees standing in for a garden
City trees patted into the pavement
And across the way the student residence
Trainers hanging from window latches
Milk cartons cooling outside on ledges
Almost close enough to touch

NOT A PRETTY SIGHT
SUCH A MESSY LOT

And you always tidy in your ways
Poor ragamuffin students
And their stinky takkies

IGNORE THEM I BEG YOU

You shopped like a villager, like a Londoner
Elegant local
A basket on your arm, calling by the fishmonger, the butcher
On friendly terms with the florist

Peonies exploding in grand style on the kitchen table
Lucy the hairdresser confiding her hard life
Eclairs and tarte tatin from the patisserie for tea
For the tiger who came to tea

HUSBAND COMES HOME WITH TICKETS FOR THE OPERA

Friends beating a path
Bicycle clips, bunches of daffodils, scarves
Earl Grey in the brown pot
Bought from the rack outside the haberdasher
Or ironmonger, or maybe the blacksmith
Could have been the vicarage
Un salon de thé
Cab engines ticking over outside
Mary Poppins in her endless descent

So far from the southern hillside garden
Greengrocer delivering trays of guavas
The van from Grove Provisions puttering laden up the drive
So far from your downtown office
Your daily colleagues

THE PERIPHERY
THE CENTRE

Can it hold?
You are held between both

On two stout sticks, two wooden legs
Your neighbouring giant clacks along the pavement
Battle of Britain hero
Dance aficionado
Like a rough beast
We watch from an upper window
Respectfully bowing

CAN WE JOIN
CAN WE JOIN
OH CAN WE JOIN THE DANCE?

I used to sit on windowsills
My body narrowed to fit the space
Sideways on like a hieroglyph
Above my bed, the wind raking the curtain
My vision locked on the horizon
Sometimes my legs dangling over the ledge
Second story legs and the small idea of falling

By day, a view of treetops
Sometimes in sunshine
Sometimes in Venetian verticals of rain
By night, a shifting wink of light

In summer, sheet lightning playing toktokkie over
the Magaliesberg

Once I shared my night with an owl
I woke to its soft hoot

I rose up on my sill
And it was there, on the roof beside my window
Tufted ears in silhouette
Its eyes wheeling towards me through the darkness

SIGN POEM 12

Our first house
The first spring tide
I called you at work
Please tell him it's urgent
They called you out of a meeting

The tide had flooded the fields
It was like a lake
A container ship passed our third floor window
Eyeball to eyeball
Like watching a city slide by
Horses kicking up on the opposite shore

Is this what you called me for?
Sounds lovely but I can't talk now

I was the over-excited city girl
Halfway across the world from an unwatered city

Zoo Lake
Wemmer Pan
Emmarentia Dam
The Wilds

IS THAT THE BEST YOU CAN DO?

Don't mock
It was the best we could do

Come to think of it
There may have been some tiny spruit
Some little fontein near the highway
Storm water drains

AT THE VERY LEAST WE HAD STORM WATER DRAINS

Don't count those
Didn't children die in storm water drains?

You came home to low tide
The river sunk to a casual slick
A quick lick along the dry lips of its banks
I was no longer quite able to explain
The exact dimensions of my fervour

Two years later
Our second house
I call you again
Get you pulled from a meeting
Please tell him it's urgent

Our boy
Little asthma lad, struggling with every breath
The big bed heaving with his chest
Ambulance or husband NOW says the doctor
Husband
You come NOW

His chest is doing the work of ten men
Ribs sucking in the whole room
Diaphragm pulling down the curtains

We get him there
Double doors open on the double
Jungle Book cutouts on the wall

LOOK SWEETIE

We had watched the video this very day
How could I not have seen?
Wheezy singing of the old songs
The penny dropping at last
Running out of the house
Looking for doctor, neighbour, anyone

At the hospital we point to the pictures
They get the mask on, the drip in
We say dinosaur names
He lifts the mask, panting

MOWGLI
TRICERATOPS
BRACHIOSAURUS

He smiles at the nurse
He wants to tell her everything he knows

MUSTN'T TAKE THE MASK OFF, MY CHAP

It takes hours for his breathing to ease
I spend that night on a chair beside him
We take turns
This is not quick
Days pass
Home and back, hospital and back
Home becomes the recliner chair
You bring me the basics
A colouring book
Toothbrush in a bag

THE BARE NECESSITIES

There are worse stories around us
Much sadder beds beside us
But I twist saddlesore on the chair
My heart twisting at the memory

WHAT IF

In the dim ward, a nurse writes quietly at a desk
My boy is asleep under his mask
His nebuliser bubbles and sighs
My hand tests the subsiding peace of his chest

ALMOST BETTER, MY CHAP

We're allowed home, we lucky ones
Back from the jungle
Carried in on the incoming tide

I can look at the view again
Him, you, the house near the river
The simple bare necessities
A list of dinosaurs as long as your arm

SIGN POEM 13

First time I came in at sunrise
Dropped at the gate by a someone
A person of the male persuasion
After a night of something
Was the first time I saw you cry

The dewy morning toiling up the long driveway
The stepped rocky shortcut
My feet lifting me over the rise
Under the trees
The sky sifting through the reds to find pink

You were at the study window, looking out
Waiting for me
My jaunty walk slowed
Heart hitting hard where it hurt
You had left the front door open

I walked slowly into the room
Dewprints following me across the wooden floor
Your eyes red
Eyes meeting eyes

WHERE HAVE YOU BEEN?

Girl's eyes met mother's eyes

I WAS AT A PARTY

My eyes down
Your eyes red
Your voice small

I WAS SO FRIGHTENED
I DIDN'T KNOW WHERE YOU WERE

My eyes red

I'M SORRY

So grownups cried

The worst thing to do to you
Crying in your arms
Girl child lost and found

The next time was that time
Hmm let's see
We'll draw a veil over that time

FOR THE TIME BEING

And the time after that was in these times
Illness washing in invisible layers
Something awry
You dropped a dish
Your hands let go though your brain held on
Tearfully you bent to pick up the pieces
Two of us coming over to help

To pick up the pieces
We wanted to reverse the action
Put the dish together again
Smooth the ragged edges back into perfection

To pick up your tears and put them back in your eyes

SIGN POEM 14

In a hospital bed somewhere near Waterloo
Somewhere near places you liked
The National Theatre
The Hayward Gallery
The river and so on

You there for tests

I THINK I MUST BE DYING

Don't be silly
Of course you're not
And that was certainly true

BUT I DON'T KNOW WHAT'S WRONG WITH ME

And we didn't know

A barrier was coming down
The jungle burgeoning inside you
Sleeping Beauty behind the palace gates

THERE'S SOMETHING BETWEEN ME AND THE WORLD

Presenting yourself at the border
All present and correct
But your passport mislaid

SIGN POEM 15

Did cave children want to talk about their day?

Lift schemes
Mothers sharing shlepping duties
Urban geography piled us together
Up and down the avenues
A mother asking: HOW WAS SCHOOL?
A daughter answering: AWFUL
Or was it: FINE ?
Homework? STACKS
Day after day after month after year
I'm not speaking of myself
I tried to give chapter and verse

Now my own children:
FINE, STACKS, AWFUL, YES, NO, CHOCOLATE

It's universal
Our homo sapient inheritance
Further back
Australopithecus

HOW WAS IT?
OKAY I SUPPOSE

SIGN POEM 16

I think it was you
The author of many a shaky super eight
The lens trembling and skidding around the subjects
Me trembling now at the sight of us then
And sick from the seasick eye of the camera

I have to stop for a bit
Lie down and count to ten
Count my blessings from one to ten

I commence watching again
Again I lean forward to see
Coalescent granules of the past
The endgrain of babyhood
Childhood tottering forwards on the screen
Speeding forwards and backwards
The Charlie Chaplin past
Its toes turned out

ONCE UPON A TIME

You were the auteur
This was the director's cut
Before you slipped away back to your study
Closed the door
Picked up briefs in pink legal tape
Spoke thoughtfully into the little machine
Silver and black Dictaphone

Wrote on pads with your gold Cross ballpoint
Serious work on serious matters
People bringing you trays of tea

KNOCK KNOCK
COME IN

But your mind making space for us
Hardly ever cross with us
Though cross with the terrible government

You came back out of the study
Picked up the camera
Turned it on us
Then we turned it on you
And we danced in a circle
And all fell down
And got up again
Covered in dry yellow grass

The screen fills with beach scenes, pools, gardens
The baby me eating sand at the lagoon
In and out of family arms
Grandparents plumped round a paddling pool
Sweet attentions from big sister and brother
They dash off screen, return
Run, climb, dance, ride a bike
My baby self reaches for them
They give me a passing pat
Like time

WHERE IS THE PAUSE BUTTON?

Big brother, satchelled, capped
Knobbly knees
Climbing into a car, tooth missing
Gets driven away into his future
Big sister riding a horse through some waves
Both ponytails swinging
Little brother heaved up the drive in a wheelbarrow
I walk helpfully beside him
He tips over backwards
I stay upright

The camera jumps
I'm in a white dress
Jean Seberg haircut
A girl in a brown dress hands me a present
Almost as big as me, in special paper
The present reveals a doll
So hideous I have to gasp

I gasp now, I mean
Watching now
Though I smiled at the time
Commendably well-mannered
I am impressed with my little long-ago self

What happened to the doll?

A SPARTAN HILLSIDE
WOLVES

Next the Acropolis
Movie camera whirring
You walk down the steps
Combed, dapper, smiling
She sits on an ancient stone
Dark haired, smiling, blooming
A Greek summer
And none of us around

THIS NOW REMINDS ME

My own Acropolis
A weekend in Athens
My brother and I
Holidaying teenagers, a little bored
Parents' siesta in the hotel
We broke out into the hot afternoon
Made a foray to a newsstand
Foraging for Europe in Syntagma Square
The eyes of white stockinged, pompommed soldiers
Slip past the tourists
Up towards the hills

ROLL THE CAMERAS

Drachmas changing hands
The booty carried back
Reading together on the floor
All those years propped on elbows
With Archie, Asterix, Superman

Forbidden Enid Blyton
And now Homer?
Not exactly
Playboy nymphs frolicked under our gaze

Who was the still unravished bride of quietness?

This is what we gleaned:
Aeons of history
The Oracle of Delphi
A wistful waiter watching along the cobbles
Moussaka and retsina
Ancient stones and amphitheatres
The money shot

Magazine smuggled successfully through customs
(The nerve rack of South African customs)
The man in the khaki safari suit smiles
Nice kids

WELCOME HOME
GENIET DIE DAG

And to you too, Meneer
My eyes meet my brother's
His friends will be so happy

FUCK YOU VERY MUCH
IT'S LEKKER TO BE BACK

Adults round a pool
The camera panning wildly

AN UNRELIABLE NARRATOR

A hotel somewhere
Malawi, Swaziland?
Couples beside the pool
Swimming costumes, open shirts
Women pull down straps
Men rub cream into shapely shoulders
Eros in the men's hats
The women's lips
You must have all wanted each other so much

NOW THAT WOULD MAKE A GOOD MOVIE

It's a movie I want to watch
But it jumps and twitches
Tracks her walking under umbrellas
Along the shore of an African lake
Then jerks back to the Johannesburg lawn
A grandmother carrying a baby, a dog gambolling

Somewhere north of the border
An imagined story unspools

THE BUMPING, WHIRRING IDYLL CONTINUES

A bar mitzvah
A remembered dress
I sit on a lap, pretending to swig wine
Whose lap? I can't make it out
You pull back to turquoise swimming pools
Girls and women in flowered rubber caps

NAIADS AT THE SPRING

Brown sister in a bikini
My Miss South Africa
Agile skinny brother somersaults onto a lilo
These days he somersaults with gravitas into taxis
Travels the clapping centres of the world
But those days he climbed highest of all in the big tree
Rode a bike with no hands
Carried a painting of a cello out of some French doors

Sister and brother on branches above me
Leoparding through the afternoon
Me in a bouncing contraption
Fat legs waving like sea fronds
A reassuring hand from my chic mama
Sultry cat on the grass beside me

THOSE JASMINE-SCENTED DAYS

Long summer days in chlorine-scented nylon
Upside down in my blue costume, I dangle from a jungle gym

Grandmother ascends a rung or two
Auburn beehive and the expected cigarette

QUITE THE OLYMPIAN

Little brother stuck on a metal outcrop
Too small to climb down

The camera catches you mowing
Handsome man in the shorts of yesteryear
I watch from my checked towel
As you clean the pool filter
Little brother skimming leaves with the gardener
Light and dark hands on the metal handle
Bougainvillea petals, scudding beetles, dowsed crickets
All skimmed gently from the surface
Like cleaning a lens

We dived for hours into the blue eye of the water
Our sword hands reaching down for the thrown stone
The coin
Circles expanding in ripples
Sun cooking the bricks
Grapes squeezed directly from the vine into our mouths
Baruch atah adonai
Blessed are you Lord our God
Something something
Who gives us the fruit of the vine

DIONYSUS AND APOLLO AT DELPHI

How did we become who we became?
So joined up
And not only in the digital splice
What centrifuge separated us
Threw us to the winds?

WHAT COULD WE KNOW?

Swept into the mouth of the camera
Spat out into the world
All the futures still coming
Fate staying its hand

SIGN POEM 17

Trying to write something tonight
I'm scanning my inner world
With a child at each elbow
Also hard at work on screens and paper

They have things to ask me
Tilt things to show me
I try to concentrate on my dream world
But it's so difficult

One of them shows me a girl
A model we'd seen
The other wants to know
Do I not find this sweet:
A cat-faced hippopotamus

SIGN POEM 18

Dark evening
Aslant in a chair in the dark kitchen
Through windows and skylights
I try to catch the night in the round

Planes blink amid the stars

I make out shapes in the garden
The studio roof
The sputnik barbecue
Trees make diagrams for the planes
They draw on the napkin of the sky
Here's how you get from A to B
North to South
East to West
The pilots check their instruments

STRAIGHT ON TIL MORNING

The undercarriages reflect life on earth
Their shifting lights echo lights on the river
Red and green signals flicker on the flat calm of the water
An unseen channel mapped
Downstream in the darkness
The sea awaits its sons and daughters

One of the planes catches my thought
Takes it on its wishbone

Carries it over European landfill
To make landfall with the African continent
Shaped exactly like itself

PLEASE HAVE YOUR BOARDING CARDS READY

For some time now the geese have been gathering
Hustlers at the water's unravelling edge
A pit stop on their road trip through heaven
Cool dawn wakes us to their flap and call

I READ MUCH OF THE NIGHT AND GO SOUTH IN THE WINTER

Daily, nightly, I tread the boards
The boardwalk, the promenade, the jetty
Looking eastwards
Like Marlow at anchor on the *Nellie*
Light thickening and darkening over Gravesend
Estuary flooding outwards to the sea
The yacht swinging on the tide
Light surging and dimming on the Essex marshes

LOOKING INTO THE HEART OF LIGHT

The darkness
The silence
We share this at any rate
Remembering and misremembering Africa

SIGN POEM 19

The man's voice on the phone

DO YOU KNOW WHAT THEY SAY?

His voice cold and furious
He tells me
Words I cannot write even now

SO THAT'S WHAT THEY SAY, HEY?

The phone slammed down
My hands shaking
I stand in the room where I played out my childhood
My childhood all played out now

In this room we played board games
The dice arcing in flourishes
Snakes and Ladders
The dice rattling in their cup

RATS' FEET OVER BROKEN GLASS

Adrenalin and emotion cornered me here
Dice rolling under the table
Back down to zero
A butterfly awaiting its pin

We built houses in this room
Wood, lego, perspex, cards
They fell down and we started again
I watched a cat give birth to mice
Made a coffin for one in a shoe box
Buried it under the cypress

I learnt to sew and forgot
And learnt and forgot
Fooling around with spools and bobbins
Patterns, pinking shears

In this room of cupboards, easels
Gramophone, sewing machine
The button box
Dressing up box
Eventually, at last, a TV
Books, a leaking beanbag
Hard and easy, hard and soft

In this room a man's voice on the phone
Rips away the parachute silk in which I float
Princess on the hill

WHO THE FUCK DO YOU THINK YOU ARE?

I feel like the newborn rat-kitten
Ugly, bald
Too weak to live

SIGN POEM 20

Girls' voices rise up through the floor

SSH GIRLS, KEEP IT DOWN

Happy voices of girls early on a Sunday morning
The birdlike ten-year-olds, up at first light
Such hopeful, uncomplicated energy
Hopping on the happy branches

HOT CHOCOLATE ON A TRAY

Girls upside down on the sofa
Laughter frothing and blossoming from them
Their foaming bursts of joy

CA SUFFIT, MES ENFANTS

When I was ten
I was ten once

WHAT OF IT?

My first camera
Bad pictures of good people
Mother on the grass
Brother in overalls
Hyena in Botswana
Myself in black and white

Anxious mug on the greyscale
But actually often laughing
That kind of laughing you long for later

A holiday in Natal
My clever friend, her dad, a dog or so
Towels on an off-season beach
Our bikinied rumps not quite risen
Cakes not quite baked
We examine each other sceptically
Both green-eyed but not jealous
Still young uns
We look down the empty beach
Vague figures approaching

(IT'S THE WOMEN WE WILL BECOME)

The day cools a bit too soon
Sugarcane knotting our teeth
Around us the delirious green
Natal's crazy richness, mangoes, avocados
Questionably humid

I'M A HIGHVELD GIRL
GIVE ME A DRY MARTINI

Back at the bellavista house for sundown
Snatches of sea through the trees
Damp cotton scraps hung on railings to dry
Suppertime moths slapping at the lights

Nightfall in girlhood's twin room
Shortie pyjamas and mosquito repellent
Her father half-poached on the whiskied porch
The two of us pretending to read quietly

Something set us going
We laughed so much
That we fell out of bed
First she fell
Then I fell
The floor indulgently meeting us halfway

WHAT ARE YOU SAYING?

I have nothing to add
The night melted around us
That's it

SIGN POEM 21

Word play
It's a human need
The mouse muse
The love vole
The pilot who loses an eye
Finds the plot
Sacred are the scared cedars

Oh my little mouse muse
Oh my little love vole
The violet violence of violins
Inviolate

The tired old heart
Showing its spider veins

Scared of the sacred cedars

SIGN POEM 22

You know what it's like
Old people getting so tetchy on buses
Morning after common morning the old gents
Harrumphing at me like billy-o

SHE'S STILL IN HER PYJAMAS
STUPID GIRL

The bus ticking at the stop
Not overly concerned

KEEPING US WAITING
AND STILL IN HER PYJAMAS

This was true
I was often late
Running down the drive
Along the road
Stapling the pages of myself together
The bus waiting patiently

But they weren't my pyjamas
They were yours, striped
Rescued from raghood
They hung big on me
Just the way I wanted

I ascended the bus
Strolled past the tutting codgers
Jailbreak student cocking a snook
I took my place at the back
My heart thundering in defiance
The blushing defiance of a stupid girl

In Hillbrow the two chaps got off
Double breasted suits and a big white moustache
Military bearing
A three-legged race to a marching band

THERE THEY GO

AFTER YOU, COLONEL
NO, AFTER YOU, I INSIST

I watched double breasted in my single breasted pyjamas
A girl kernel in a soft shell
Jailbait hermit crab
Scratching at the dirty glass
Your fatherly armour saved me from their scorn
Mother of pearl buttons deflected their arrows
Their crosspatch bullets

The thing is maybe they were nicer once
And of course I sometimes wore other things
Almost normal, not worthy of comment

Your pyjamas are gone but I still have you
We sit together on the tube
We watch undercover as women set to work
Making it up as they go along
Mascara and blusher
Eyeliner's miraculous sweep

Shameless
Hanging on the mirror's every word

SIGN POEM 23

Why is it so very difficult?
Writing words about Africa
Impossible
The impossible dream
The task rejects me

YOU ARE NOT FIT TO TOUCH THE HEM OF AFRICA

Spoiled girl
Lazy woman
Can you ever say the right thing?

SIGN POEM 24

I am familiar with platforms
I catch the London train again and again
To see you

A horizontal journey
(This is Essex we're talking about)
Though sometimes the clouds form mountains
We are hurtling towards Tibet
Shangri La the next station stop

The anticipated scenery is there again
It unrolls before or behind me
Depending on which way I'm facing

Is knowing where you're going better than knowing where
you've been?

All the unwindings, carrying us onwards
Bias binding, fire hoses, cables beneath the sea
We are slipping off a reel
Reading ahead while our mouths struggle with speech
Nuts in our cheeks for the winter

Imagine if London was on top of a mountain
You caught a funicular up the steep slopes
Coming up from a lakeside station
You stepped out into the clear air

In a trance
The city contained in a nutshell

I catch the train again and again
To see you and you and also you
But mainly you

SIGN POEM 25

One day, some years ago
Not sure how far back
We are gathered round a fire
Another Johannesburg winter
The cold descending with the sunset

You sit in an armchair with the cat on your lap

THE CAT IS ON MY LAP

Here I presume to give you back your voice
I should not
But I do

You read aloud from a travel book

I CAN STILL DO THIS
ZIMBABWE
VICTORIA FALLS

The cat stretches and purrs
You slump back on the pale green velvet
Slowly you close your eyes
We are left in the room
Excluded from the world behind your eyelids
Trying to guess where you've gone
The page in the travel book unclear, turning blank

THE CAT
THE HOLLOW SPACE
WHERE IS THE WORLD?

The room is filled with talk
Pine cones and logs are added to the fire
The smell of resin fills the room

I RING
THE ANSWER COMES:
YOU HAVE BEEN DISCONNECTED
PLEASE TRY AGAIN

SIGN POEM 26

Early summer
The greens still fresh
Bright white clematis climbing the fence
Fox terrier asleep in the sun

The sound comes down the muffled road
It's the cut-short bleat of the ice cream van
Always just around the corner
Something about it chills me
I don't mean its cold, sweet load

Those few notes slice through the afternoon
Stopping, then resuming
The sound music but not music
A ventriloquist's puppet music
The creepy attempt at play

Like those books of fairy tales I never liked
Pages to be hurried past with a shiver
Otherworldly stories where nothing was safe
I preferred a place where nothing happened

JUST LET ME DO MY FRENCH KNITTING

It's the living fairy tale
The broken musical box
Pied Pipering through the estate
Hansel and Greteling in the closes
Up the snicket and down the lane

SIGN POEM 27

First year English, sun falling on the desks
Our tutor reading Chaucer aloud to us
Most of us following in our books

WHAN THAT APRILLE WITH HIS SHOURES SOOTE

I look around

THE DROGHTE OF MARCHE HATH PERCED TO THE ROOTE

John, in the seat parallel to mine,
Is looking at Jane, sitting in front of me
These are not their real names

His mouth is actually open
His eyes cannot tear themselves away
The tutor reads on

AND SMALE FOWLES MAKEN MELODYE

Enunciating the famous words

THAT SLEPEN AL THE NIGHT WITH OPEN YE

Unexpected sounds explode from her practised lips
Embarrassed, admiring laughter from ours

Jane half turns
She looks at John
He looks at her and so do I
What hand made her?

SO PRIKETH HEM NATURE IN HIR CORAGES

Mascara smudges, thick kohl
Blue starlet, starlit eyes
Breasts stretching her inadequate shirt
I am almost as entranced as John
Something pricketh certainly

THAN LONGEN FOLK TO GOON ON PILGRIMAGES

The tutor asks something
Without moving his eyes from Jane
John's hand shoots up
He answers brilliantly as always
Jane's heavy lashes blink slowly
Their stoned, fluttering weight almost too much for her lids to bear

What page are we on?
Her rumpled bedroom whisper
John reaches across to show her

AND BORN HIM WEL, AS OF SO LITEL SPACE

His arm burnt on contact with her breast

IN HOPE TO STONDEN IN HIS LADYE GRACE

I know she is not for him
He knows it too, in Middle English spelling
His stout pilgrim heart stumbles perhaps

She is the stuff of myth
Not for him her sleepy mermaid call
An engineer approaches in the corridors

SIGN POEM 28

My friend brought me a bucketful of roses
Now they burst out of clear glass
Smelling like heaven itself

IT'S SUMMER, IT'S SUMMER, IT'S SUMMER

I sink my nose into the bowery scoops of their petals
Sucked into their soft whirlpool
I drown, beelike

SIGN POEM 29

One Paris night
Lights strung down the hill
Fish-stalls still open
I am looking at the hypothermic crabs
Waving gently from their icy beds
My plastic-wrapped, supermercato eyes are in love

From a side street café, an ordinary place
A woman steps off the step
She catches me passing
Shouts in my face
Catches me in the wind of her madness

ARRETE, ARRETE

Does she mean me?
Must I stop?
I hurry on, though taken aback

MADAME, MADAME

Her old voice harsh, cracked
Debris swept into a running gutter

Two days later, she is there again
Morning coffee in the square, croissants
My boy and me

The lost one wandering under the chestnuts
Still wanting to arrest the world

MADAME, MONSIEUR

Harsh, urgent
There is something she needs to impart
A waiter actually wields a broom
What does he see?
A nuisance, worse than the pigeons
But what does he know?
Her life trailing behind her
The steam of her story rising from her hot core

Courtesy chasing sanity
Grabbing at the conveyor belt
Blister packs of meaning just out of reach

STOP I SAY
ARRETE

A grand old lady once asked me:

WHERE DO YOU STAY WHEN YOU'RE IN HONG KONG?

Oh my dear Madame
I was a sunburned girl of seventeen
I summered in the hothouse of my hoping heart
Overwintered in the reed bed of my booklined boudoir

Truly, my dear lady

THEY KEEP A ROOM FOR ME AT THE MANDARIN ORIENTAL

My special gin on that secret shelf behind the bar
Tonic flown in from Rio
My table placed in just the spot I like
Overlooking the harbour

I laugh now in wonder at who she thought I was
How I perhaps appeared to her
A fine girl
A good family
Au fait with the maitre d'
Also little cats e, f and g

AND HOW WILL MADAM BE PAYING?

I laugh at the idea but not at her
Her world reached for mine
Tried to meet me on a soft paisley carpet
Strolling out from behind the potted palms
Outside, the glittering water
Sampans, cormorants, junks

JOKES ASIDE

I think of my neighbour
Six foot tall

Dutch Resistance
Sailor, gardener

She has been gone a year
Her shade, though, returns
Bumping down the road on her bike
Courgettes from her allotment, raspberries
The pannier full
Knocking at our door with offerings

Two doors down, the key hanging behind the bench
Indonesian shadow puppet over her bed
Her blacksmith father's candlesticks
Retsina in the fridge
New frailties
Sometimes we had hands to catch her, sometimes not

On roller skates, perfectly balanced
One Cyd Charisse leg extended endlessly behind her
She flew in the photograph above her chair
Its white wicker held her in her last years
Her long stride stopped by falls

Days now measured by something beyond an inner will
Seated at the window
Morning and afternoon the scrabble of schoolchildren
A book of crosswords
All year round the opening of buds
A windowsill of daffodils, roses, cyclamen
Polar bears on TV

On certain days visitors came
They arrived unexpectedly
A dirty little man in her bed
Children singing on the stairs
Rabbits in the light fitting

PLEASE WILL YOU ASK THEM TO LEAVE

At the last, a baby abandoned in the road

PLEASE SAVE IT

Bending to catch the Dutch words
Dredged up by fever
From that deep place where the oldest self meets the youngest
89 years of being only herself

What we have is an inner impossible logic
The waking dream in all of us
Tenuously, tenaciously we hang on to what we hope is real
What we fear
What we believe we know

HONG KONG. THE NETHERLANDS. PARIS

We have the postcards to prove we were there

SIGN POEM 30

It's like seeing the curvature of the earth
Watching you sleep in your Clubworld pod
Pink jersey slightly moth-eaten
The knot of your tie rising above the v-neck's ribbing
Your old scarf in silky folds on the wool

I look at you across the seat divider
My hand is in yours
I want you to be there always
The fact remains
It should be someone else holding your hand
But I'm here instead, keeping her place

ORLANDO THE MARMALADE CAT
AND HIS DEAR WIFE GRACE

Your white hair is still thick at the sides
Green eyes, the loving diagonals of your lids
The same smile as in those little boy photographs
Its unchanged sweet line

I leave the plane and look down on you from space
You have the shape of a father
And also something so big
I take precise measurements
As best I can (my shaky geometry)
Yours is the shape of a lifetime and of the earth

SIGN POEM 31

Some days ago
I lay on an oak bench
Looking up into the heart of a birch tree

It was a moment taken from a morning
Snatched from an adult's hurly-burly morning
Driving, thinking, performing

THIS REQUIRES INTERPRETATION
THIS CRIES OUT FOR INTERRUPTION

The dog dealing with grass-roots matters
Children in dialogue with cereal boxes
Computer screens, shower heads

THIS REQUIRES YOUR ATTENTION

Five quiet minutes I needed

Walking across the mossy, damp lawn
I wanted to sit just briefly on the new bench
The oaken plank balancing under the birches
And when I sat, it came upon me:
I must lie down
So I did, lengthening myself along the knots

I was taken up into the white, birchy bark
The fine branches spreading high above me
Delicate leaves of finest, saw-toothed green
Everything high, delicate, engulfing
An adjacent tree spilling bunches of red berries
The sky visible through tangled tracery
Everything dappled

Lying on my slab
I was lifted off the earth
The sky was the earth, the leaves the air
My hands crossed on my chest
As I levitated between earth and sky

In my mind I brought you here
I knelt on the damp grass
I wanted you to lie here and see what I saw
You were on the bench in my mind
But first I had to help you unfurl
Trying to be gentle, I placed your head where mine lay
I straightened your legs
Your feet pointing towards the house

YOUR HOUSE

Your arms, so stiff; the unyielding fingers:
I unbent them very carefully
I stroked them back into the picture
They became pliant and flexible
Your servants as of yore

I straightened them at your sides
(Was I your servant or you mine?)
Then crossed them over your chest
(As mine were crossed then)

Your body relaxed into the bench
And you could look up
(In my mind your vision was clear)
I wanted you to see what I saw
Hear it

Soundings from feathery leaves
The garnets spilling through from the neighbouring tree
Some sky and clouds
Insects buzzing
Doves softly calling

(At night these birches host owls)

High up, a small plane left its trace

I lay and you lay too
In flickering green light
On a hard, perfect bed of wood
Narrower than a truckle

Five lone minutes trickled through my fingers
I wanted to stay all day
But I was summoned
I pretended not to hear

MUM

Just one more minute please

MUM, COME

I waited another beat

I'M COMING

All that day and every day since
My mind has dallied under the birches
Sometimes it is just me
Other times you
Me kneeling there
Lifting you up
Soothing and smoothing you down

SIGN POEM 32

With my mind on other things
My eyes come to rest on the floor
There are proteas in a vase at my feet
A spray of japonica, water

We had no truck with proteas in the old country
By we I mean us
Reactionary flowers
Carried by people waiting at the airport
The old building, flat, dull
And the proteas the same
Great fans of them, in cellophane jackets
For people stepping off the old planes
A rough, ugly simper of welcome

Now I see them through fresh eyes
My friend's Hawaiian eyes
She knew them on her dot of land
Floating in the Pacific
Like ginger flowers
Like hibiscus
Rare, precious, remarkable

I'm looking hard now at my proteas
Watching them
Her threefold gift
They thrust forwards like curious birds

Like microphones
Waiting for the message
The next song
They seem forthright here, in this English room
In cooler light
Generous with their time
Set in a cold English window
They bring a sense of a dry veld landscape
Of course pine cones, artichokes, thistles
Overlapping woody, dusky petals
A southern hillside set with aloes
But something also from the lush tropics

Now I understand what my scoffing young heart did not
My eye-rolling, shrugging young heart:
From the protea-toting tannies and their suited men
I get it now:
Arrivals deserve ritual
What the airport flowers said
Like Hawaiian leis
Hello. You're here. We're happy

SIGN POEM 33

Something surprised me yesterday
Red-hot pokers growing in an Essex garden
What were they doing there?
I thought they belonged south of the equator
They belong on a koppie with a baboon nearby

GET YOUR FACTS STRAIGHT FOR HEAVEN'S SAKE

I once had strep throat
My fever so high that you dreamed you were in a desert
A red-hot poker stoking my throat
My fever stoking your dream

We brought out the extremes in each other's dreams
You in a burning desert
Me in an ocean that had no end
I could not swim across it
A boundless, drowning ocean

When I woke up
You brought me clear, clean water from your oasis
Sunlight slanted across the parquet
We washed sand and salt from our stinging eyes

SIGN POEM 34

His body in disarray
Like something shaken up in a bag
On the way home from the shops
Man or boy?
I couldn't say
Arranged on the pavement
Arms, legs, elbows, feet
Nothing in the right place
A bag of bones thrown together by a witchdoctor
A suitcase of a human
Badly damaged in transit

BUT TO WHOM COULD HE WRITE?
DEAR SIR, I WISH TO COMPLAIN

He was uncomplaining
I remember him smiling and talking
I think he had a companion
Someone must have helped him
Assembled him on his spot under the portico
Because there he was

DAD, WHAT'S WRONG WITH HIM?
THE FRIGHTENING ERRORS OF THE BODY

On the pavement,
Cardboard for a cushion
We put coins in his hat

Visiting you at work
Up in the lift to the Sixth Floor
Past the receptionist
The secretary
Past other lawyers who made comments
Shook your hand
Nodded at us

We followed you into your chambers
That grand word

A KING'S WORD

A wood panelled room
Bookshelves full of law reports
No novels here
Your big desk, some big chairs
A medieval woman looked at us from her panel
Dark eyes in a worn gold frame
And we looked out of the recessed windows
Supreme Court pillared across the road
Advocates in gowns crossing the road
Collared

We tried to find him below us on the pavement
But the angle was wrong
He was under the portico

We jinked about while you gathered papers
Ready for the next thing

A milkshake?
Or a gingerbread man from the OK Bazaars?

Back down and out
Past the bundled man-boy
I drew away into the life you gave me
And here I still am
But where did he go when night came?
Who looked out for him?
What happened to him?
There must have been some human pleasures

THOUGH HE'D BEEN TRAMPLED BY A MONSTER
Crumpled

He had a name which we never thought to ask
All of us there in the same unfair space
Locked apart in the sugared afternoon
Worlds almost impossible to mention

SIGN POEM 35

When your baby looks at you with cocktail eyes
You've had it
Your goose is cooked

Those eyes, newborn, gazed at the lights
The first-time world
Her new kitten eyes roving in wonder

Now in a Paris bar, we order drinks
They bring open-mouthed glasses
Maraschino cherries
She passes me hers, I eat it
The mother's duty
The mother's reward
We bend over a book
Plan our next moves

It's late
The glass exhales its vodka sigh
But her eyes, those almond shapes, are wide
Their blue light shining out
Parisian heads turn in wonder

SIGN POEM 36

My twenty first summer
My heart so broken it tolled and rattled with every step
After managing well enough in Pisa and Lucca
All had collapsed in Spain
Pain chewed me to a pulp
Trudged me through the hot towns
The trains, the arid plains, the refrain

HE LOVES ME, HE LOVES ME NOT

My friend and her serviceable Spanish getting us through
Cheap biscuits and cerveza
Families with their grandmothers
Podgy babies lace-socked in the jolting carriages
I clung to the sticks of their laughter

FORGET ME, FORGET-ME-NOT

Finally, the lowest moment
Food-poisoned and grief-struck in Alicante
Heart-sick, gut-sick
Losing it amongst the elegant compadres
Promenading at dusk along the avenue
My friend dragged me groaning up the road
In and out of palm-frond shadow
Back to the poor pension

Dog-sick and sobbing,
I curled in night's cobweb

ALL COME TO NOUGHT

But I was young
The aching, eternal knot could untie itself a little
In the morning, for instance
I shook off the bug
Made my heart tight
(Bandages, wallpaper glue)
Patted myself down
Hoisted myself up

OR SO I THOUGHT

And in the morning, for instance
The sea came knocking
Spain came calling
We found friends
Sweet peppers
Americans
The geraniums of Seville
A fiesta

SIGN POEM 37

Naming things became so important
Walking in gardens
Names of flowers and trees coming thick and fast
It was a way of keeping your feet on the ground
Keeping your finger on the pulse of the known world

BUDDLEIA, PHILADELPHUS
JAPONICA, CEONOTHUS

Keeping the oxygen of words circulating through your blood
We walked round the big garden
Keeping to the path
I repeated your words
Both of us trying to hold the names

WILLOW, TULIP, BROOM
JASMINE, SNOWDROP, SAGE

The trees stroll past us, the shrubs
Moving in the opposite direction

SIGN POEM 38

Moulded leather from Italy and London
Emissaries from New York
Your still, elegant shoes occupy their shelves
They have suffered no melt-down
They remain intact in their essentials
Still elegant

I took over your brogues
So now I walk in your footsteps
I make your footprints
Your heels worn low in a slightly alien slope
My stride compensating
Me a 37, you a 38

NEAR ENOUGH IS GOOD ENOUGH

It is like a child walking on its parent's feet
That game we all played
The parent walking the child
The kid steering its personal robot
Feet planted on living stilts

PUT YOURSELF IN MY SHOES
LOOK AT IT FROM MY PERSPECTIVE
(You might have said)

In your brown lace-ups
I walk the streets of the world
For you and with you
Since you no longer can
I wear clothes of yours, jewels
I like to have you close
Whether you know it or not

SIGN POEM 39

How strange the things that stay with us
The slight hauntings that keep pace with the years

DO YOU REMEMBER THAT UNFORTUNATE INCIDENT?

(Girls, I am talking to you)
(Boys, look away now)

I AM TALKING OF THAT TIME
REMEMBER?

Whispered: blood on the sheets
Hissed, behind the hand: that time
Oh, THAT time

Yes, the beautiful sheets
The blood
The barely known man
His pristine sheets
The midnight flit
The flight
My mind flinches at the memory
The perfect rose, the perfect snow
Thread count way above normal
From the banks of the Nile
The man so stunned with displeasure

AND NEVER ANOTHER CALL

What wisdom do we gain?
I wish I had, I wish I hadn't
The should and the shouldn't
It wasn't love
I wish I hadn't

SIGN POEM 40

This morning, golden
Full of winter roses
Yesterday the bones of the rain

This morning a barge pulled away from its wharf
The river gilded, flat, pure
The barge filled to the gills with glittering grit
Flat-topped containers lined up on deck

THEIR SMOOTH GEOMETRY

MY HAND A VISOR
FILTERING THE GLARE

The riverside quarry spoke its ancient language
Its mounds humming in the light
Rinsed pyramids and sand dunes
A mountain range to charm a jaded eye
The old cranes like printed spires
A scaffolded cathedral in the local sky

KEEP LOOKING, DON'T TURN AWAY

I stopped and looked into the sun
Watching the barge slip downstream
So quiet and serene
The water holding its weight with godly strength

My mind conjured visions

Photoshopped images, surprisingly specific
Sent them across the current
To the containers' receptive length

AN EMPTY PLINTH
TWO SHIMMERING HOLOGRAMS

On the one hand, Cleopatra
Straight-backed on a shining throne
Sphinxes and leopards guarding her feet
Her black-rimmed eyes fixed on the horizon
The waters parting before the prow
Shore birds hushed

THE WHOLE MORNING ENTHRALLED

In the other picture, Nelson Mandela
(These were his funeral hours)
What was coming;
Motorcades, tanks, marching soldiers
Sombre-suited speeches, cameras
Helicopters, prayers

WHAT I SAW

His bier carried on the barge
The English river standing in
For aloes on a southern hillside
The green rolling hills of home
His long coffin draped in a flag

Or maybe just air

THE HEAVENS' EMBROIDERED CLOTHS
My mind's fingers sewed a misty cloth of gold

Curlews paced at the water's edge
While I strained to see til the very last bend
A vessel, a coffin, a man's face
Accompanied by a queen, a sphinx
Some leopards

SIGN POEM 41

The business of catching a dream
Is an inexact art

CONCENTRATE THE MIND
EMPTY THE MIND
FORGET IT

I'm wading in a rushing stream
Orange fishes are flashing past
Laughing under the sparkling water
While I plod and lunge
Like a grizzly floundering in a Canadian brook

FORGET IT
CATCH US IF YOU CAN

The fishes are flashing me
Their rude little bodies slipping through my hands
It's very difficult
The water running high between its banks
Droplets splashing up
Green fronds bending down
Lilies, leafy tangles above me
And I am wet and the fish are laughing at me

THE BASTARDS

So I sit on a rock
My feet dangling in the non-stop water
At last a fish bites my toe
My mind holds its breath

GREAT
HERE IT COMES

The fish leaps up
That thing – the tiger, the bus – it shouts
You know, and the staring girl?
Now do you remember?

SIGN POEM 42

In the lift, I straighten your collar
Imitating her instinctive, familiar gesture
Tender, exasperated
My hands, like hers, brushing down the lapels
Tidying your pocket flaps

An elegant stranger
Squeezed into the little box with us
Regards herself in the mirror
Her jacket is padded silk
Her black shoes gold-buckled
A certain kind of woman
From a certain kind of London

I feel briefly embarrassed
Having called attention to your unkempt collar
But then I see
Beneath the line of her grey bob
Her cashmere polo-neck is askew
My fingers itch to right it

SIGN POEM 43

I needed to renew my poetic license
A form arrived
Boxes were ticked
They required a photograph
I affixed one of the dog
He is quite the English Romantic
In his all-weather coat, he tramps the countryside
Gazes at grass stalks
Barks at the wind
Then ambles home like Wordsworth
To a dry biscuit

SIGN POEM 44

SWALLOWS DIP OVER THE BRIMMING RIVER

Walking home from the station I stop to watch

SHADOWS OF OLIVE LEAVES ON THE WALL

The river a lagoon
Its high tide lapping at the houses

THE ADMIRAL'S HOUSE, THE BOATYARD

And I have left you to come home
Back to the village, the family, the dog
My abandoned studio

It is election day so I stop to vote
Polling booths in the village hall
My name crossed off the list
I think you will not be here next time I vote

THUMBS UP IF YOU HEAR US

You are weakening
Your thumb is faltering
But lifting still: you hear us

You have been inside your illness
Like a flame inside the mouth of a tiger
Pinioned in its cruel embrace through these years
Longer than we thought possible

SUPERWOMAN IN YOUR WEAKNESS
YOUR NAME STILL ON THE LIST

One Sussex supper
Word games and family stories
We chose words to describe one another
One word per person
His word for you: REBEL

A rebellious beauty all your life
Even now, head back on the pillows
Your delicate face
Wedding ring on a chain around your neck

Candle in the tiger's mouth
Burning and flickering like the lamp in the temple
Burning for eight days instead of one
Magic oil keeping destruction at bay

Flame
River at high tide
Everything you have ever been and known
Pooled inside you like a lagoon
All the greens reflected, and the clouds

THE STREAM OF CONSCIOUSNESS
THE STYX

A river running clear over stone
Hummingbirds fluttering among the reeds
Swallows skimming the water

SIGHS, LAMENTATIONS

You are your own mythic chorus
Wellspring of your own story
Lamp, wick, river, rebel flame

CODA
7 June 2015

Hummingbirds fold their wings
Morning glories close their petals

Hummingbirds close their petals
Morning glories fold their wings